This book is dedicated to all who find Nature not an adversary to conquer and destroy, but a storehouse of infinite knowledge and experience linking man to all things past and present. They know conserving the natural environment is essential to our future well-being.

GRAND TETON

THE STORY BEHIND THE SCENERY®

by Hugh Crandall

Hugh Crandall, since his retirement from the Navy in 1960, has contributed much toward helping Americans understand their national parks. He lived and worked at Yellowstone National Park for several years as interpretive consultant to the National Park Service and as director of the Yellowstone Institute. His familiarity with the neighboring Grand Teton National Park has enable him to bring to these pages a great appreciation for and knowledge of this rugged but friendly park.

Grand Teton National Park, located in northwestern Wyoming, was established in 1929, to protect the Grand Teton Range and the lakes below.

Front cover: Beaver Pond reflections, photo by John P. George. Inside front cover: Chipping sparrow. photo by Erwin A. Bauer. Title page: Elk resting, photo by Franz J. Camenzind. Pages 2/3: Winter sunrise over the Teton Range, photo by David Muench.

Edited by Mary L. Van Camp. Book design by K. C. DenDooven.

Ninth Printing, 2004 • New Version

The valley of the Tetons is a land whose very
essence is mountains. No one who has walked
among the spires of the Teton Range, who has seen

*its peaks rise out of the morning mists or loom in mystery
against the evening sky can ever forget the spell of timeless
majesty these rugged mountains evoke.*

The Grand Teton Story

The Snake River, aptly named, winds through the valley floor below the namesake peaks of the park. Autumn is just one of the times in the year where this view becomes a spectacular sight to witness.

JOHN P. GEORGE

Grand Teton National Park is a massive work of art. It is also the studio in which it was created and the gallery in which it is displayed.

Like any large, complex art work, Grand Teton is composed of thousands of individual details, of themselves suitable subjects for study and admiration. Even the part of the composition which is the studio-gallery contains details that are nearly as arresting and rewarding as the mountains for which they provide the setting.

Without question, the splendor of the Teton Range is the most impressive aspect of the Grand Teton masterpiece. It is a splendor so magnificent that our perception of it must expand to encompass senses other than just the visual. We may, then, also compare the scene before us to a symphony—a symphony whose major theme, the Teton Range, is so enhanced by minor themes and grace notes that ultimately even features as awe-inspiring as the Cathedral Group and Mount Moran must be accepted as only details in the total creation.

That major theme—the young, precipitous mountains of the Teton Range—might well have towered much higher above the valley called Jackson Hole over the nine million years they have been forming, were it not for the inevitable process of erosion. And in the past 30,000 years or so, the principal erosive force was montane glaciers, huge masses of ice and rock that scoured the stream valleys into *U*-shaped troughs and carved the mountains into cones and ridges with concave slopes. It is this glacial carving that has made the Teton Range so esthetically inspiring.

A shoveler duck swims in the peaceful waters of one of the many lakes and river. Grand Teton is a major stop over on the north-south migration routes.

the scene opens up before you like a symphony in full string...

Although the great impact of Grand Teton National Park is as a single composition, it may be regarded as having four distinct elements —again, a symphony, whose four movements are the mountains, the lakes, the valley, and the river. Each joins and overlaps the others, yet each retains its own identity. It is left to us who visit the Tetons to appreciate these elements in our own ways, and with our own sensitivities to mix and blend these rich strains into a composition that has meaning for each of us.

Time and the forces of earth have created a glorious harmony here at Grand Teton. With experience and understanding, we can perceive this masterpiece with all our senses and enjoy to the fullest all that it has to offer.

Horsepacking is popular in Grand Teton, but the rugged terrain makes much of the mountain area inaccessible to these animals. Horses have a serious impact on fragile wilderness areas, and care must be taken to minimize their effects.

The Mountains

As mountain ranges go, the Tetons are fairly insignificant, statistically speaking. It is a small range, about 40 miles long and 15 miles wide, and its peaks are not very high. Only 7 are higher than 12,000 feet, and of these only the Grand Teton exceeds 13,000 feet.

But the emotional impact of the Teton Range cannot be experienced by reading statistical data. One must *see* these spires which seem to rise straight up out of the lakes at their bases—so whimsically that they have been called "the mountains of a child's fables." Millions of people, brought here by the highway that lies just across the small lakes from the mountains, have felt the aura of fairy-tale magic. Only on second thought do most of us begin to wonder how all this beauty actually came about.

The reality is a story of its own, a story of geological events and change: The crust of the earth—the solid rocks and soil on which we live and on which the oceans rest—is not very thick. And it is constantly changing. The changes are not always obvious, because they usually take place on a time scale that is so much longer than that by which we eat and sleep and keep appointments and count birthdays. Never-the-less, when the poet refers to "the unchanging hills," he is exercising his license to exaggerate. *All* hills change, especially the high ones, the mountains.

They change because the forces that lifted them are still working to lift them even higher. And they change because the counter forces of erosion are continuously working to make them lower. The earth is constantly uplifting and eroding, creating and destroying. It is like an artist with many ideas and only one canvas.

JOHN P. GEORGE

The Teton Range is one of earth's latest efforts, "painted" only recently over the landscape that previously occupied this part of the country. Whereas most of the Rocky Mountains were created at least fifty million years ago, the forming of the Tetons began about nine million years ago, and it may still be going on.

The geologic process that created the Teton Range is called "faulting and uplift." It is one of the three basic ways that mountains are made, and it happens like this:

The crust of the earth sometimes cracks into large blocks (in the case of the Teton Range, proba-

The peaks of the Grand *Teton Range tower above the autumn color giving us a vivid contrast to the elements of the park. Above the treeline, no forest exists. It's just too cold, windy and harsh to support anything but sparse ground cover. The fall season provides for both vacationers and photographers who always look for that "perfect picture."*

bly because of tension exerted by continental drift), the way ice on a lake cracks into floes. When that happens, each block is free to shift, relative to the adjoining blocks. It can move up or down or slide sideways. Often a block will tilt, one edge rising while the other subsides.

The Teton block lies from roughly the Idaho-Wyoming border to Jackson Hole; its eastern edge has been rising for nine million years. Another block lies from the eastern foot of the range eastward into the Mount Leidy highlands and the Gros Ventre Mountains; its western edge has been sinking. During all that time the two blocks have been moving against one another—one rising and the other sinking—through sporadic earthquake producing jolts. The accumulated movement has been about six miles, mostly in the sinking block.

While all this has been going on, the agents of erosion—wind, rain, running water, grinding ice, freezing, and thawing—have also been at work, wearing away the high places and leaving the worn-off material in the low areas. Today the difference in elevation between Jackson Hole and the Grand Teton summit is about 7,000 feet.

The uplift has been uneven because of the manner in which the Teton block has been lifted: rotated upward as if hinged at its western edge, much like a trapdoor, so that the eastern edge has done most of the rising. As a result, the eastern face of the Teton Range is high and very steep, whereas the western side gradually slopes downward into the Teton Basin in Idaho.

The tilting uplift has resulted also in an unusual location of the water divide of the range. Every mountain range has a divide—the meandering line that marks the places at which raindrops, on reaching the ground, separate to flow down opposite sides of the range. The Teton divide was established millions of years ago when the uplift began. From a line passing along about the high eastern edge of the range, some streams flowed down toward the west and the Teton River, and others flowed eastward toward the Snake River in Jackson Hole, the valley that was formed by the subsiding of the western edge of the adjoining block.

Because the eastern side of the mountains was steep, its streams were fast-flowing and had more cutting power than the slower streams of the more gentle western slopes. Since they thus eroded the rock faster, they were able to cut through the crest of the range and capture some of the drainage of the streams that flowed westward. Over the centuries, this process gradually shifted the water divide of the Teton Range westward to its unusual position well below the highest elevation.

That process has slowed, probably because the continued rising of the block has steepened the western side and the gradient, or slope, of the eastern streams has been reduced by their own erosive action, so the divide may not shift much farther, if any. Large mountain glaciers later widened steep, water-cut gorges into broad, U-shaped canyons where streams now sweep and cascade. The deeper canyons that separate the magnificent peaks of the eastern escarpment of the Teton Range have made these high summits even more spectacular.

Another unusual feature of the Teton Range is the vast difference between its age as mountains and the ages of the rocks of which the mountains are composed. Most of the exposed rocks of the eastern face of the Tetons were formed about 3 billion years ago, which means that the mountains have been shaped, in part, from rock that is at least 300 times as old as the mountains themselves. If you climb the Tetons, or even handle the boulders of the talus slopes at their bases, you are touching rock that is two-thirds as old as the earth itself!

In the case of a mountain that is formed by volcanic activity, molten rock is poured or blasted out onto the surface, and as it accumulates into a mountain it also hardens into rock, so that the age

Springtime brings out the best in floral color. The grasses grow. Life springs into view. The cycle repeats year after year.

DAVID MUENCH

The west side of the Cathedral Group, viewed from Table Mountain, displays the dramatic results of glacial erosion.

DAVID MUENCH

The town of Jackson lies at the foot of East Gros Ventre Butte, an outcrop of igneous rock in Jackson Hole. Giant glaciers overrode this hard rock but did not level it.

of the mountain is the same as the age of its rocks. But the Tetons were formed by a different process, one that results in a strange paradox wherein the youngest mountains of the Rockies are largely composed of some of the oldest rocks in North America. How did this come about?

The ancient gneisses and schists of the eastern face of the Tetons are metamorphic rock that is believed to have once been igneous rock (molten material that cooled and solidified) and sedimentary rock (fragments that were deposited in layers and then solidified)—material that lay under an ocean near a chain of volcanic islands. These deposits were buried deeper and deeper as other layers were deposited above them. Eventually, as the weight of the overlying rock became greater, they became semifluid under that pressure and the heat it generated. Their minerals were chemically altered, and the arrangement and alignment of their crystals were changed; thus they became metamorphic rock with new and different forms. This all happened about 3 billion years ago, and it is this rock from which Mount Moran was later shaped.

At the time of metamorphosis, this rock was probably the deepest rock in this part of the earth's crust. Later, during the general uplift that formed the North American continent (or some other, even older, land mass that is no longer intact), they were stretched and cracked. The molten-rock material below them was forced into the cracks and cooled into solid rock. The earliest known of such

These peaks happen because nature is at work—constantly at work. Mountain building goes on at an unseen pace. Winter with snow and ice create the expansive forces that take the mountains down – in chunks and blocks. What are left are those tetons, those Grand Tetons.

intrusions occurred 2.5 billion years ago and is evident today as layered gneisses, which often contain flaky schist and pegmatite, a rock with the same mineral composition as granite but with much larger crystals.

A billion years after the first intrusion (or about 1.3 billion years ago), the whole mass of rock, including the dikes formed by earlier intrusions, was once again cracked. A different molten material was forced into the cracks and hardened into a type of rock known as *diabase*. The most obvious example of these later intrusions is the "Black Dike," a wide, vertical band which bisects the upper face of Mount Moran.

Capping the Black Dike, like the crossbar of a T, is a thin layer of sandstone. It is all that remains uneroded of about 3,000 feet of the sedimentary-rock layers that can be seen on the west side of the Tetons and in the mountains across Jackson Hole to the east. Its grains were once sand that lay on the floor of a shallow sea that covered what is now Montana and Idaho, and most of Utah

Earthquakes will move mountains, But so too can imagination.

Mount Moran looms above the Oxbow Bend of the Snake River. In the center of its steep eastern face is Skillet Glacier, one of the many small true glaciers of the Teton Range.

and Wyoming. It was compacted into rock about 500 million years ago.

Because the western slope of the Teton Range has eroded less than the high eastern ridge, it still retains a sheathing of those sedimentary deposits. Their *actual* ages—from the 550-million-year-old *Flathead Sandstone* formation to the 330-million-year-old *Madison Limestone* formation—can be determined with considerable accuracy by radioactive dating. Their *relative* ages can be determined by paleontologists by analyzing the many plant and animal fossils they contain.

As the deposits were laid down, grain by grain, organic remains were embedded in the sand and silt. Paleontologists, who know the particular period of time in the distant past in which each species lived and thrived and know the conditions of environment that were necessary for the support of each of those ancient organisms, can infer the nature of the world in which some particular plant or animal lived and died and left its leaf or shell or skeleton as a record.

The layers of rock, although tilted by the uneven rising of the Teton block, are still in the order in which they were formed. The oldest is still on the bottom and the youngest is on the top. But there are gaps of many millions of years in the record as told by the Teton rocks. Some of these gaps once may have been filled by material which has since eroded away, but most of them represent times when the land rose slightly and the shallow sea receded and no new material was deposited.

The original material was deposited in horizontal layers and the rock into which it has changed is banded in those layers, sometimes thousands of feet thick. Sedimentary rock can be seen from the valley floor on Rendezvous Mountain at the southern end of the range and in the central part of the range by looking up Avalanche Canyon. The bandings of the several layers can be seen clearly by looking southwest from a point across the Alaska Basin or by looking south from the top of the Teton Village tramway. The present sloping of the bands downward toward the west demonstrates the trapdoor tilting of the Teton fault block.

H*ikers can cross* the divide between Indian Paintbrush and Cascade canyons.

A CLIMBERS PARADISE

If you do hike to Alaska Basin, you'll find that the Tetons present a different and much more intimate aspect from that seen from the valley floor. Once you are actually there amidst the Tetons, you find a world of extremes—tiny lakes and towering cliffs, wildflowers and awesome chasms, delicate waterfalls and jumbled masses of boulders. At lower elevations the landscape seems to be made up of rock, trees, and water. At higher elevations, even the hardy firs and whitebark pines cannot be sustained; instead there is the low vegetation of the alpine, where much of the water is ice, snow, or glaciers during most of the year. Above treeline only the rock remains the same.

To the trail hiker and backpacker, the Teton Range may be perceived as three parts: From the south boundary north to Paintbrush Canyon the mountains are laced with clearly marked, well-maintained trails. From the north boundary south to Webb Canyon there are also trails, but they are often primitive and are minimally maintained. The central section, from Webb Canyon to the southern end of Leigh Lake, has no trails. It can be walked over, but it isn't easy. The cliffs are often too steep and the stream beds are usually choked with huge rocks and fallen trees.

To the mountaineer, the Teton Range again presents a different facet of its personality. Few mountains have seen as much traffic or have been enjoyed by as many climbers. There are three reasons why the Tetons—and the mountains that encircle Yosemite Valley—have been the two principal American centers of climbing for many years. First, the rock is hard and tightly fixed and is therefore secure and forgiving of small errors. Second, they offer a wide range of climbing experiences, from merely a hard walk uphill to a highly technical climb that can challenge a master. Third, and most important, they are temptingly displayed and very accessible.

The Teton summits are not as easily reached as the Yosemite cliffs, but they are very climbable. It is often said by mountain climbers that they accept the challenge of a particular mountain because "it's there." True, the Tetons have been there for the many thousands who have climbed them, but, more than that, the Tetons have been *right* there. Climbers, for all their great health and strength and endurance, can be as lazy or as short of time as the rest of us. Most of them would prefer not to have to walk several miles before beginning to climb.

As might be expected, all the peaks and spires of the Tetons have been climbed, most of them by several routes. Today, records are kept of the ascents which are reported. Registering for each climb is no longer required, though back-country permits are necessary ot camp overnight. Climbing was not always as controlled as it is now. A person who is driven to challenge himself, as most mountaineers are, is often subject to whims of the moment, leading him in new directions. So there have probably been many ascents in the Tetons of which we know nothing.

Most of the "firsts" have been recorded—even those which took place during the early history of the area. But the only first ascent that has ever been of any particular concern to the climbing community has been that of the highest mountain here, Grand Teton, and that ascent has been the subject of dispute ever since it was first claimed.

In 1872 the Hayden Expedition, the second expedition to explore the Yellowstone country, was split into two groups. One group, under Hayden, went north to Bozeman and reentered Yellowstone by way of the route of the earlier exploration. The other, under James Stevenson, set out to explore the area south of Yellowstone. According to the official records of the trip, the party was on the west side of the Teton Range in late July, and on July 29 several of its members set out to climb the highest peak, Grand Teton. Two of them—Stevenson and Nathaniel Langford—reportedly made it to the top.

Nothing that is known of Stevenson's character or that can be inferred from his report of the climb offers any reason to doubt his claim. Nevertheless, one man, William O. Owen, perhaps eager for fame or driven by a sincere but unsound conviction, chose to dispute the Stevenson—Langford claim in published statements that were unreasonably acrimonious and frequently inaccurate. He himself had failed to reach the summit of Grand Teton in seven attempts, beginning in 1891, and had finally succeeded—under the leadership of Franklin S. Spaulding—on August 10, 1898. His efforts to discredit Stevenson and claim the first ascent for himself resulted in the passing of a resolution by the Wyoming legislature in 1929 which substantiated Owen's claim. Bolted to the rock on the summit of Grand Teton, a heavy bronze plaque proclaimed this opinion—until the plaque was stolen in 1976. Like some other past legislative actions, that one was never entirely endorsed by the people, most of whom prefer to believe that the credit for the first ascent belongs to Stevenson and Langford.

Many have followed the route of that first climb to the top. These people have had the satis-

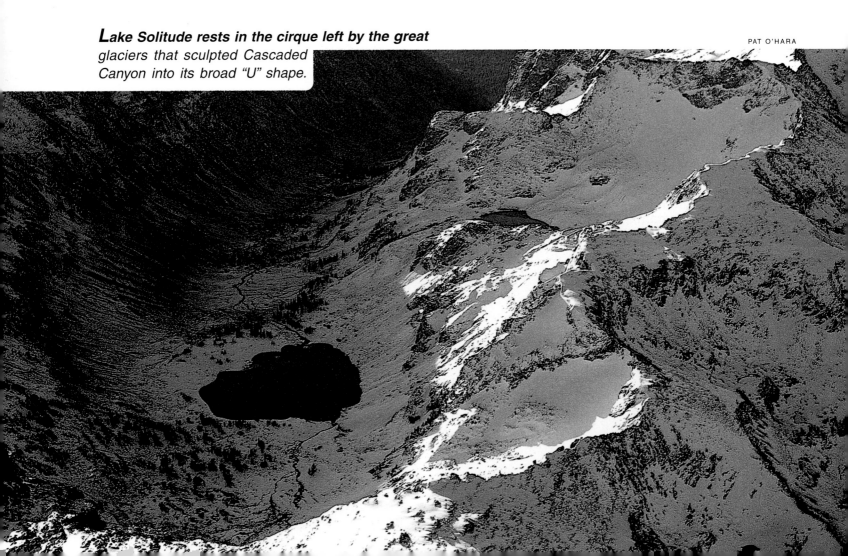

Lake Solitude rests in the cirque left by the great glaciers that sculpted Cascaded Canyon into its broad "U" shape.

PAT O'HARA

A climber, poised on the Middle Teton, contemplates the steep walls of the Grand Teton.

ED COOPER

faction of having tested themselves and triumphed, and they have had the reward of a magnificent view in all directions. At 13,770 feet, they have stood on the highest point of land within sight—and on a clear day that's a lot of land! Only a small percentage of those who come to know the Tetons have the privilege of standing on the crest of the highest mountain. But most of us are glad these few are able to achieve that particular pleasure. Meanwhile, we find our own rewards in other ways and in other parts of the rich variety that Grand Teton National Park offers.

SUGGESTED READING

KLOBUCHAR JIM. *Where the Wind Blows Bittersweet.* Wayzata, Minnesota: Ralph Turtinen Publishing Co., 1975.

LOVE, J. D., AND JOHN C. REED, JR. *Creation of the Teton Landscape.* Moose, Wyoming: Grand Teton Natural History Association, 2003.

ZIM, HERBERT S. *The Rocky Mountains.* New York: Golden Press, 1964.

We climb because it feels so good when we stop.

*Great glaciers were the dominant
erosional force in sculpting the Teton Range,
Jackson Hole, and the surrounding
skyline into today's scenery.*

The World Created by Glaciers

While glaciers live, they move. Sometimes they advance as tongues of ice, flowing slowly and ponderously down stream valleys. But even when they seem to be at a standstill, they are moving within themselves. Snow falls and packs at their upper ends. Its weight and the natural fluidity of ice cause the snow to slump slowly toward the lower end of the glacier, where it runs off as glacial melt water.

Embedded in the packed snow are particles of rock that have fallen from the mountainsides or have been plucked by freezing from the rock walls that enclose the glacier. When the ice melts, the bits of rock are deposited at the glacier's terminus, as if at the end of a giant conveyor belt.

As the glacier becomes smaller, fading away during very long periods of warm or dry weather, its leading edge recedes in an uphill direction from the crescent-shaped mound of material its conveyor- belt action has piled up. The water from the glacier's continued melting is thus dammed behind the mound of debris and a pond is formed which grows to a lake as the glacier continues to shrink. In the south fork of Cascade Canyon, along the trail to Alaska Basin, there is an example of this process in action—a textbook example so typical and complete that it has been called "Schoolroom Glacier."

THE LAKES

Formed in the same manner, but less obviously, are the lakes that rim the base of the eastern escarpment of the Teton Range. This necklace of lakes—Jackson, Leigh, Jenny, Bradley, Taggart, and Phelps—is the result of the final dwindling of the last large glaciers which occupied adjoining canyons and gouged out the depressions which the lakes now occupy. The terminal moraines of those glaciers are now the low, tree-covered hills that separate the lakes from the lower land of the main floor of Jackson Hole.

South of Jackson Lake, the five smaller lakes—from Leigh on down to Phelps—remain intrinsically undisturbed by man, although there are developments along the eastern shore of Jenny Lake, an inholding (privately owned land within the park) at the south end of Phelps Lake, and trails that lead to all of them. Only these five lakes were included within the boundaries of the park when it was first established in 1929.

Jackson Lake, the largest of the six, differs from the others in that it does not receive all its water from nearby mountain streams; its principal source is the Snake River as it drains the southern section of Yellowstone. The Snake is also the lake's only outlet as the river continues southward through Jackson Hole. Originally, Jackson Lake covered an area of about 17,000 acres. Then, in 1906, the lake's outlet was dammed by private interests as an irrigation venture. That dam washed out but was replaced by the Bureau of Reclamation

Not only can we enjoy mountains by looking up, but also with all the lakes, ponds and rivers in Grand Teton, the reflections can be just as dramatic as the "original." If it were not for the tree branch, you could hardly tell the difference if you viewed this image upside down!

DAVID MUENCH

The Jackson Lake of today, which extends to the base of Mount Moran, is really a reservoir that impounds the melting snows of spring for summer irrigation in the Snake River Valley of Idaho. But under the top 39 feet of water lies the ancestral Jackson Lake, on whose shores people made their summer camps for thousands of years.

as part of the Minidoka Reclamation Project to control the rate at which the Snake supplied irrigation water to the farms of Idaho. After the dam was raised in 1916 and the outlet channel was dredged in 1917, the maximum depth of the lake was raised by 39 feet and its area increased by over 8,000 acres.

For its administrators, management of Jackson Lake is a continuing "tightwire act," in which they must balance the interests of the differing segments of the area's population. The oark and the Wyoming Department of Game and Fish are concerned with maintaining the level of the lake and the rate at which the river flows in a pattern as close to normal as possible in the intertests of preserving the scenic value of the lakes and their use as an optimum habitat for the wildlife of the waterway. The people who live in southern Jackson Hole are concerned with preventing the potentially destructive flooding that can occur in spring and early summer. The farmers of Idaho are concerned with ensuring that they will receive an adequate supply of water to meet their irrigation needs. These various requirements are not always compatible. No one really envies the local officials of the Bureau of Reclamation the job of keeping all their customers happy.

During years of normal precipitation and dam operation, the system has been worked out to the satisfaction of nearly everyone. By late June, Jackson Lake has been allowed to fill to its maximum surface elevation of 6,769 feet. By mid-September, after meeting the summer water needs of Idaho farmers, the level has gradually dropped about ten feet. Outflow is then adjusted to equal the inflow until the spring melt begins and is allowed to restore the lake's depth to its maximum level. Adjustment is sometimes necessary to allow for unusual spring flooding that may be anticipated. In years of heavy snowfall, the additional drawdown may amount to another eight to ten feet.

In years of abnormal drought, however, the spring melt may not fill the reservoir to capacity. During such years, 2002 for example, summer requirements are unusually large, and the drawdown of the impounded waters may reach its maximum of 39 feet. At those times, the water level is so low that the shallow areas which sustain the bottom-rooted plants and limnoplankton—the basis of the lake's aquatic food chain—are left as unproductive mud flats, and the marinas at Colter Bay and Leek's Landing are rendered largely unusable.

Jackson Lake was not part of Grand Teton National Park until 1950, when Jackson Hole National Monument (established in 1943) was incorporated into the park. At that time, a few conservationists opposed the expansion because it

would incorporate the artificiality of the "Jackson Reservoir" and the "Snake Irrigation Canal." Every 15 or 20 years, when extraordinary control measures are required and the artificiality becomes apparent, it may be conceded that these "purists" were perhaps right. But in the inbetween years, the park may accommodate as many as 50 million visitors who will not be aware of the river's unnatural flow.

The two other large lakes in Grand Teton, Emma Matilda Lake (named for the wife of William O. Owen) and Two Ocean Lake (mis-named by someone who must have thought it straddled the Continental Divide), were formed during the last ice age by enormous glaciers that flowed westward into the valley from high ridges to the east. Actually, glaciers mostly shaped Jackson Hole and its encircling mountains during this ice age, which ended about 12,000 years ago. Recent field investigations have led glacial geologists to reject previously published names and dates of glacial periods. New evidence suggests that in this part of the Rocky Mountains the last ice age began about 30,000 years before the present,

The Gros Ventre River meanders
through glacial deposits as it forms
part of the boundary between Grand Teton National
Park and the National Elk Refuge.

and great glaciers of this period were the dominant erosional force in sculpting the Teton Range, Jackson Hole, and the surrounding skyline into today's scenery. Valley lakes relect not only dramatic vistas but also the geologic history.

Grand Teton's lakes are ringed by forest. The soil at the foot of the mountains and in the moraines which form the other boundaries of the lakes is rich in minerals and fine enough to hold water. So, unlike the gravelly outwash plains, those areas can support trees. Most of the trees at the elevations of the lakes are lodgepole pines. But as elevation progressively increases up the mountainsides, the lodgepole pine gives way to subalpine firs on the slopes, spruces beside canyon streams, and-near the 9,000-foot treeline-whitebark pine.

Because of the trees and because Emma

Matilda and Two Ocean are farther from the mountains than the other six, their appearance is closer to that of north-woods lakes than of alpine lakes. A visit to these lakes, then, can be a welcome relief to the visitor who finds himself overwhelmed by the constant presence of mountains. Emma Matilda Lake is accessible only by walking but there is a road to Two Ocean Lake, and a small picnic ground lies on its northeastern shore.

Although Jackson and Jenny lakes are used for boating, the principal contribution of the lakes to Grand Teton is of course their scenic beauty. The lakes constitute one of the minor themes which unify and complete the Teton composition. And on days when the wind is still, they reflect in their mirror-like surfaces the major theme—the awesome Teton Range.

Showy fleabane

The **lakes** of Grand **Teton** are one of the minor **themes** that **unify** and **complete** the **whole** Teton **composition**.

THE VALLEY

The work of glaciers involves more than the artistic carving of rocks into spires, pinnacles, and knife-edge ridges. Like the sculptor at work in his studio, a glacier eventually has to do something with the unused byproducts of its labor.

As long as a glacier has strength and volume, it carries these byproducts along as it slowly flows downhill, even using some debris as tools to help in the cutting process. But, as a glacier shrinks and weakens, it gradually discards its load of boulders,

A *few ranchers, former owners of land that is now parkland, retain grazing rights for their cattle.*

Freezing fog crystallizes on dried grass and transforms it into fairy wands.

DAVID MUENCH

ED COOPER

Oxbow Bend glistens in the icy beauty of winter. The southern portion of Jackson Hole lies in the rain shadow of the high peaks of the central Teton Range; consequently, snowfall and rainfall are not as heavy as in the northern part of the valley.

gravel, sand, and rock dust. Geologists have given names to the various types of "debris piles" left by glaciers: glacial erratics, lateral moraines, terminal moraines, outwash plains, kettles, etc. Just as the story of the active life of a glacier can be inferred from the shapes of the rock it has worked, so the history of the final days in the life of a glacier can be read in the pattern of those deposits.

The floor of Jackson Hole, 400 square miles of glacial debris, is land on which such a history has been recorded.

Jackson Hole apparently has been something of a valley ever since the time about 9 million years ago when it began to subside and the Teton Range began to rise. From time to time, several different large lakes have occupied the present site of Jackson Lake. But the final shaping of the valley and the mountains was begun only 30,000 years ago and was completed just 12,000 years ago. The final tool the sculptor used was ice.

The glaciers which developed in this area were not part of the vast continental glaciers that covered most of Canada and large areas of the north-central United States, although they existed at the same time. These mountain glaciers formed

here because the land was high enough to have the same cold climate as the lower land farther north. During a lengthy glacial period that predates the last ice age, ice, deep enough to cover all but the highest peaks of the Pinyon Peak and Mount Leidy highlands, flowed southward from the Beartooths and the Absarokas and westward from the Wind River Range. It filled the entire valley and flowed out the southern end and on into Idaho. It covered and shaped Signal Mountain, Blacktail Butte, East Gros Ventre Butte, and West Gros Ventre Butte.

When the 2,000-foot-thick mass of ice melted away, there was little soil left in Jackson Hole. Most of it had been scraped or washed off and replaced by a thick layer of quartzite cobbles and pebbles.

Overleaf: *Evening reflections, Jackson Lake. Photo by David Muench*

Fireweed

Sulphur buckwheat

Scarlet gilia

Evening primrose

Glacier lilies

In the parts of the valley which were not subsequently covered by later glaciation, this gravelly layer, usually covered by sagebrush, has strongly influenced the present uses of the land by man and other life forms.

Periods of glaciation are often followed by abnormally warm, dry periods called *altithermals*. They are caused, to some extent, by a lack of plants—plants which would normally shield the bare ground from the baking of the sun and dampen the atmosphere with their transpired moisture. During such dry periods, smaller rock particles—dust and sand—can be transported for miles by the wind and redeposited elsewhere. Many of the best and richest soils of the world have been formed from windblown dust.

Layers of such material, called *loess*, range from less than an inch to several feet in thickness and are interleaved between the layers of outwash gravel and glacial till in Jackson Hole. Except for the small pockets of silt found along old stream beds, these layers make up the only really good soil in the valley. They also provide sites for many coyote and badger dens, probably because the material is easily dug, doesn't quickly turn to mud when wet, and is stable enough so that a hole in it doesn't cause it to collapse.

By the end of the last ice age, the finishing touches had been added to the shapes of the mountains and the topography of the valley, and the terrain looked essentially as it does today. The last chip had been removed from the mountainsides; the last shaping had been done to the stream valleys; the last lake had been impounded; and the last load of debris had been dumped on the floor of Jackson Hole. Jackson Lake had become water instead of ice, and the Snake River was developing a new channel through the new land surface. The last of the ice lay in half-buried lumps on the level surface south of Signal Mountain. Soon it too would melt and leave the "knob and kettle" formation now called the Potholes, that would be the last work of the dying glacier. It was time for the area to begin to accumulate inhabitants.

Plants moved in, then plant-eating animals. Man, who ate both, followed closely behind them. But, for 12,000 years after the glaciers had left, man was only a summer visitor. Most plants and animals are severely limited in their choices of habitats, each having its own specific requirements for life support. Some organisms became permanent settlers here; others tried the area and then moved on.

Only sagebrush, coarse grasses, and a few herbaceous plants found the gravel beds of the outwash plains suitable. The soil was too coarse to hold water, and what little precipitation fell from the dry air of the altithermal drained quickly through the gravel. The mounded moraines, made of finer material that held water better, were occupied by pine trees. Stream beds supported trees—aspens and cottonwoods—and willow shrubs. Cattails and sedges settled in the marshy places. Finer grasses grew on the surface deposits of loess. The plant residents in each type of terrain added their modifications to their habitats and soon recognizable plant communities became established.

*L*upine leaves

ED COOPER

*T*he geometrical precision of the salsify is repeated in the showy seed cluster, which resembles a giant dandelion.

ED COOPER

ERWIN A. BAUER

The bull elk's spreading antlers shed in midwinter and are grown anew in spring. By fall, the antlers have once again become impressive weapons with which the bull must compete for and maintain dominance over his harem.

FRANZ J. CAMENZIND

The stately antlers of bull elk outline intricate patterns against the winter whiteness. Elk have a metabolism that allows them to rest comfortably in their beds of snow.

The plant-eating animals were each attracted to the plants which best served their nutritional needs—the moose to the willows, the beaver to the aspens, and the Clark's nutcracker to the pines. They moved into these plant communities and modified them still further. Then meat-eating predators and scavengers followed their favorite foods, and each distinct combination of terrain, soil, and microclimate became a stable biotic community.

About 700 species of higher plants occur in Grand Teton National Park, and each is well established in its particular habitat. Some 300 kinds of birds and mammals have homesteaded in the park. Most of them, too, are there to stay, but some range through several communities, either in search of prey or to adjust to seasonal changes. One of them, the American elk (*wapiti* to the Indians), has been a problem to modern man ever since the settlement of Jackson Hole and the establishment of the park.

Jackson Hole National Elk Refuge is the winter range of a herd of about 7,000 to 10,000 elk. Natural food is insufficient during most winters and is supplemented by feedings of alfalfa pellets.

MARK NEWMAN/ANIMALS ANIMALS

FRANZ J. CAMENZIND

***E**lk claves are born in the spring or*
early summer and retain their juvenile spots
until they acquire winter coats in the late fall.

Elk summer in the high country and historically have migrated to winter ranges in southern Jackson Hole and possibly south and east of the valley. Today the town of Jackson, ranches, and other developments occupy much of the historical winter range of the elk and are situated across their traditional migration routes. In 1912, an elk refuge, managed by the Bureau of Sport Fisheries and Wildlife, was established northeast of Jackson. Its fences were successful in keeping the elk out of the town, but they also blocked their migration to areas farther south and east. The result is that in winter the herd is concentrated in a limited part of the original range.

On the refuge, the elk are provided supplemental food as needed. During mild winters, when the elk arrive late at the enclosure and leave early in the spring for their summer ranges, this supplemental feeding is minimal. But during severe winters, many tons of alfalfa pellets are required, particularly when the size of the herd has increased during a preceding period of mild years. Some believe that, under such unnatural conditions, successful management (holding the herd to a manageable size) may depend on sport hunting. The alternative—an occasional large die-off during particularly harsh winters—is not considered acceptable by these people, even though it is the management device that the natural world has

Moose are commonly seen in Grand Teton. Usually solitary in nature, they congregate among the willow thickets of the Snake River in summer and on the sagebrush flats north of the Gros Ventre River in winter.

practiced, including natural predators, successfully for thousands of years and would probably result in a stronger herd.

As a result of such thinking, the compromise that permitted the expansion of Grand Teton National Park in 1950 included a stipulation that sport hunting was to be allowed in the park. Consequently, Grand Teton is the only national park in the entire system in which hunting is permitted. This unusual situation is not very palatable to chagrined conservationists and people who expect total protection of wildlife in national parks. In the view of most people, however, it is better for the park area to include part of the unusual glaciated valley, even at the price of allowing hunting, than to limit it to the mountains and the five lakes which lay within the original park boundaries. Even those visitors who are less than charmed by the sagebrush/grassland community which was added in the expansion appreciate it as a platform from which to enjoy the immensely rewarding vista of mountains and river that the park encompasses as a result of that expansion.

THE RIVER

The Snake River channel, which glides through the glacial deposits of Jackson Hole, is a secluded world of swift water, swift fish, swift birds—and the slow-moving, stately moose. These elements comprise a distinct ecosystem in a world apart. Most visitors to Grand Teton get only a glimpse of the river as they cross a bridge, or they may merely infer its presence from the line of trees between them and the mountains. The people who do go down into the river's domain—to fish in it, to float on it, or just to look at it up close—may feel a sense of isolation here, a feeling of being cut off from the activities going on above them. But once they become familiar with the river, they learn that it, too, is an active world, albeit a very different one.

A fish rises to take an insect floating on the fast-moving, rippling surface of the river. Swallows skim the water, taking insects in midair. A kingfisher perches on a tree branch, an osprey hangs in the air, and the eyes of both intently: scan the river for fish. In a quiet backwater, the head of an otter breaks the surface, then sub-merges again to continue its own search for fish. A moose idly browses the willows. A beaver clambers out of the backwater and moves off among the aspen. All this goes

Canada geese nest on the low banks of the braided channels of the Snake River.

Taken in a broader view the valley floor and its autumn color provide the basic scene. The mountains serve as just a distant backdrop.

on in a narrow ribbon of green that meanders through a land of parched gravel and sagebrush.

The Snake River drops 700 feet and winds 40 miles to cover the straight-line distance of 22 miles from Jackson Lake Dam to Wilson. Along parts of its route, it has cut through mounds of glacial material to such a depth that its banks have become very high. In others it sprawls in multiple channels across terrain that is nearly flat. Its average course is south-southwest, but it flows in many directions in maintaining that course. The western side of the valley has subsided since the Snake first established its course, so the river no longer flows through the lowest part of Jackson Hole. The streams that drain the lakes west of the river have to parallel the Snake for several miles before the river drops low enough for them to enter it.

Trees have established themselves throughout most of the river bottom cut by torrential meltwaters of the ancient Snake. Spruces thrive near water. Cottonwoods and aspens cover drier areas. In a few places the banks are too steep to encourage vegetation; there the layering of the glacial deposits can be seen. If one of the layers is a band of loess, it will no doubt be a sieve of swallow holes. The coyotes and badgers aren't the only ones who can recognize good material in which to dig nests!

Where the river is braided across flatter land,

Rafting the Snake River below the Tetons is a wonderful way to enjoy a summer day and, perhaps best of all, a great way to experience both the mountains and valley floor.

-31-

Aspen trees thrive along the Snake River. They are a favorite food of beavers.

both banks of all channels support aspens, cottonwoods, and willow shrubs. In winter the willow marshes are home to the area's wintering moose population of some 600 animals, but this concentration is widely dispersed in summer, with only 200 moose staying in Jackson Hole.

Early mountain men called the Snake the "Mad River." Between the upper end of Jackson Lake and the southern end of the valley there were few places to cross it. During the spring melt-off, when it was swollen by the runoff of the thousand or so square miles it drained, it could often turn into the raging torrent that the name implied.

Today, it is controlled by the dam at Jackson Lake; excessive flooding and excessive lowering of its water levels are avoided. The Snake retains much of its wildness, but water control does render it somewhat less than natural.

If you float the river, in the course of your journey the outside world will be periodically cut off from view by the trees and high banks which border the river in places. During these times you can imagine yourself to be almost anywhere—Oregon, Minnesota, Virginia. Then you round a bend into an east-west stretch of the river. Suddenly the mountains are there, soaring upward in all their power and grandeur. There is now only one place in the world that you can be: on the river of the Tetons, in the valley of the Tetons, in the land of the Tetons.

SUGGESTED READING

HARRY BRYAN, AND WILLARD E. DILLEY. *Wildlife of Yellowstone and Grand Teton National Parks.* Salt Lake City: Wheelwright Lithographing Co., 1972.

RAYNES, BURT. *Birds of Grand Teton National Park and the Surrounding Area.* Moose, Wyoming: Grand Teton Natu.ral History Assn., 1984.

SHAW, RICHARD J. *Plants of Yellowstone and Grand Teton National Parks.* Salt Lake City:Wheelwright Lithographing Co., 1974.

The serenity of Grand Teton is shared by beavers who build their homes, by a moose who enjoys its clear running water, and by people who view the scene.

If you ride the river, the outside world will be periodically cut off from view by the trees and high banks which border the river in places. During these times you can imagine yourself to be almost anywhere

*The first humans were here
to hunt, gather food,
as well as search
for rocks to make tools.*

Before there was a Park

Humans may have first come to this continent about 35,000 years ago, passing across the Bering Land Bridge. The facts surrounding this ancient migration are shrouded in mystery. But it is known that human beings have been living continuously on this continent for at least 20,000 years.

We tend to think of the American Indians—the descendants of these ancient peoples—as horsemen, especially those belonging to cultures of the western United States, but the truth is that the horse and the mobility it provided arrived in the New World only recently, with the European explorers and settlers. The native peoples of North America had been foot travelers for all the many thousands of years that they lived here prior to the arrival of the Spaniards, only a little more than four centuries ago.

The people, then, who left their faint traces in the Teton area 10,000 years ago were hunters and gatherers. They traveled on foot and transported their possessions on their backs as they moved with the seasons to be near their sources of food and water. It would be 9,000 years before any American would ride a horse; 5,000 years before any American would cultivate corn; and 500 years before people anywhere in the world would cultivate crops of any kind! So the first humans in this area were here only to hunt meat, gather food, or search for rocks from which to make their tools and weapons.

When we speak of the culture known as "hunter-gatherers," we usually don't give quite enough emphasis to the "gathering" aspects of their livelihood. It was a rare group of primitive people who subsisted wholly on meat. Most of them augmented the frequently uncertain provender of their

DAVID MUENCH

hunters with edible plants which grew naturally—roots, fruits, nuts, leaves, and the seeds of grasses and forbs. Winters were spent in the mildest and most sheltered parts of their ranges. When spring arrived, the people moved from their winter camps to places where they could dig the roots of the camas lily, collect tender young cattail shoots, catch cutthroat trout in unfrozen lakes, and wait—comfortable and well fed—for the berries to ripen and the wild grain to head out. They also searched for

Golden grass and yellow aspen leaves in the late-day sunlight contrast with the shadowed bulk of the Tetons across Jackson Lake.

new deposits, or revisited known ones, of chert and obsidian, from which to fashion knives and projectile points, and soapstone, for bowls and pipes.

Jackson Hole provided all those things, but its winters must have been harsher than those outside its encircling mountains. No evidence has been found of any permanent settlements in the valley, although proof exists that it was occupied seasonally during a period spanning thousands of years.

A campsite discovered on the north shore of the original Jackson Lake was eventually covered by many feet of water when the lake rose after the dam was built, but not before it had been investigated by archaeologists. The artifacts found at the site revealed that it was used frequently, perhaps annually, for at least 10,000 years before historic times. Two projectile points of the Clovis type, a style of shaping that was common from 12,000 to 9,000 years ago and has since been abandoned,

WILLARD CLAY

have been found elsewhere in the region. During the time that such a projectile point would have been in use, the valley's northern end would just have been released from a cloak of glacial ice.

For these primitive people, hunting was a constant, year-round occupation, even during those months when edible vegetation was plentiful. So, during the summer sojourns in Jackson Hole, while the women and children were digging for roots, the men killed bison and other large game and hunted waterfowl among the lakes and marshes. Some of the meat was dried and a portion of it used to make pemmican, prepared by pulverizing the dried meat on grinding stones and mixing it with suet and sometimes dried berries. The pemmican was then packed into rawhide boxes or pressed into cakes for storage. Many grinding stones have been found throughout the area.

The archaeological sites found so far in Jackson Hole seem to indicate that primitive peoples made concentrated use of areas in the northern and southern sections but left a relatively unoccupied section in the middle, creating a conspicuous "buffer zone." Several factors could account for the heavy use of the northern and southern ends of the valley. The Snake River constituted a barrier to people traveling on foot except at certain places—it could be forded safely to the north where it entered Jackson Lake and far to the south near Hoback Junction. Also, the principal groups who used the valley seem to have entered it from areas to the north and southeast and thus would have been prone to settle near those entrances.

Well into historic times, the "Sheepeater" Shoshone continued to come into Jackson Hole to spend their summers. They used, among other places, that campsite at the northern end of Jackson Lake which is now under water. In the fall they returned to their permanent camps in neighboring Yellowstone, either by traveling directly north or by crossing the Tetons through Conant Pass, going up the west side of the mountains, and reentering their home territory by way of the Madison River.

It is not possible to identify any particular group of prehistoric Americans with the tribes existing during recent times. The extensive network of Indian trails, the broad dispersion of trade items (Yellowstone obsidian, for example, found as far east as Ohio), and the inter-group relationships that we know prevailed among Indian tribes at the time exploration by white men began all indicate that communication between "tribes" was always extensive and that no subculture remained truly unchanged throughout generations.

The Sheepeaters came as close to a static society as any group in the northern Rocky Mountains. They seem always to have lived as small family groups, dispersed throughout the Yellowstone area. Perhaps because they were conservative, or maybe just because they were content with their own way of life and had no desire to change it, they never acquired the horse and thus were not subject to the cultural changes that animal brought with it. They continued their traditional routines until late in the nineteenth century. Historic accounts of these people and their patterns of activity thus available to us have been helpful to archaeologists. They have permitted them to make inferences regarding the lives of prehistoric peoples in the mountain West and to acquire a reasonable understanding of the summer residents of Jackson Hole during the early post-glacial millennia.

FUR TRADERS AND TRAPPERS

Beginning in the early nineteenth century, the area around Jackson Hole saw more and more traffic by white men, both American and Canadian. There is some reason to believe that John Colter was the first white explorer to enter the valley, although many now question the claim. Whether or not the story of his expedition in 1807 is true, it will no doubt continue to be told and retold, because it was a stupendous feat of the sort that awes and overwhelms us. And it was an adventure undertaken for what in retrospect seems a trivial and improbable purpose.

John Colter was many things—a Virginian, a hunter, a trapper, an explorer, a consummate mountain man. But, when he performed this, his most noted feat of wilderness adventuring, he was working as a traveling salesman for the Missouri Fur Trading Company.

He had been a member of the historic Lewis and Clark Expedition on its epic journey to the Pacific. On the return journey, as they headed down the Missouri back to St. Louis, Colter left the expedition to spend another winter in the wilds—but as a trapper, not an explorer. The next spring he was again going downriver toward civilization when he met Manuel Lisa and a party of men who were traveling upstream to set up a trading post.

Colter signed on with their fur company and helped them to set up a base of operations—Fort Raymond on the Yellowstone River at the mouth of the Bighorn River.

In November of 1807, Colter set out from Fort Raymond to try to persuade the Crow and Shoshone Indians to the south to use the new trading post as an outlet for their furs. He started that first trip through his sales district in November, in order to reach his customers while they were in their winter camps.

He kept no diary or journal. In 1810, when he finally returned to St. Louis, seven years after he had left the frontier town with the Lewis and Clark Expedition, he probably told his old boss, Captain William Clark, about his experience. Clark kept a rough map on the wall of his office on which he recorded new information about the unmapped West, a map that has been preserved through the years. On it is a dotted line indicating Colter's route. Even allowing for inaccuracies (and the map contains several), the travels of that 35year-old mountain man during the winter of 1807-08 constitute an odyssey which can only be described as "heroic," perhaps as much so as the legendary expedition on which he had started his western adventures so many years before.

The pine marten is a sleekly beautiful member of the weasel family. It is an agile climber and a fierce hunter of birds and small mammals. As its name implies, the pine marten frequents pine forests, especially in rocky areas.

TIM CLARK

ERWIN A. BAUER

The yellow-bellied marmot makes its den among rocks.

DAN SUZIO / ANIMALS ANIMALS

The sluggish porcupine feeds on tree tissues and bark.

Piecing together the best information that is available today, it is reasonable to assume that Colter went up the Yellowstone River to Pryor Creek and followed Indian trails over Pryor Gap and down to the Shoshone River near the present site of the town of Cody. Then he went up the Bighorn and Wind rivers to cross the Gros Ventre Mountains through Union Pass into Jackson Hole. He seems to have forded the Snake River at or below Wilson and crossed the Teton Pass into what is now Idaho. On the west side of the Tetons he moved northward and recrossed the range by way of Conant Pass, then followed Berry Creek on down to the Snake River above Jackson Lake and turned northward again. After that he may have

circuited the west side of Yellowstone Lake and continued down the Yellowstone River to ford it on the Indian trail near Tower Falls. He would have been able to continue on that trail up the Lamar River and Soda Butte Creek to the headwaters of Clarks Fork of the Yellowstone and to the trading post.

It is known that Colter left Fort Raymond and we know the approximate date he left. It is also known that he returned. But no record exists of how long the trip took and there is little proof of his exact route. There are people who question whether he ever got west of the Absaroka or Gros Ventre mountains. The only bits of "evidence," other than Clark's map, are a stone that was plowed up in an Idaho potato field in 1931 and a tree blaze purported to have been found in Yellowstone National Park in the late 1880s. Some think that the stone—which has "John Colter" inscribed on one side and "1808" on the other—is a hoax, and some think that the blaze—in which a

The gray wolf is a necessary part of the balance of life in nature. At one time certain predators like the wolf and the cougar were thought to be harmful. Now we know better. – Life in balance…

ERWIN & PEGGY BAUER

Cougars serve man and nature better than we ever realized. Life in all its forms is part of a well-orchestrated cycle. Sunlight is the basic source. Chlorophyll in green plants transforms the sun's energy into sugars and starches. The plants are eaten by small animals, herbivores, which in turn serve as food for animals higher on the food chain, such as wolves, cougars, coyotes, and even larger animals like deer, elk and antelope. – Life in balance…

ERWIN & PEGGY BAUER

FRANZ J. CAMENZIND

ERWIN A. BAUER

A mother coyote stalks a mouse in the late summer grass, while her pups wait in the den. In Grand Teton, coyotes dig their dens in loess, a fine-grained, stable soil that doesn't collapse as most glacial deposits would.

large X was cut above the initials JC—was made in 1872 by the botanist John M. Coulter.

True or not, the story should be preserved, at least as legend. In the early days of the American West, it somehow seems right for this rugged man, alone and on foot, to have traveled 500 miles across some of the most difficult terrain of the Rocky Mountains in the dead of winter—just to advertise a new store that had recently opened a couple of hundred miles away!

To most of us it doesn't really matter whether Colter was the first white man into Jackson Hole. Perhaps the first was another of the 43 members of Manuel Lisa's fur brigade in 1808 or 1809, or some member of Major Andrew Henry's trapping expedition of 1810-11. Whoever may have been the first, the valley became known to many modern Americans very early in the nineteenth century.

Jackson Hole, over the next three decades, saw frequent traffic by American and Canadian trappers—frequent because it was now an explored territory, the fur trade was profitable, and opportunities existed because the exact ownership of the land to the west of the Continental Divide was unsettled. Despite legal squabbles and the interruption of the War of 1812, the fur trade prospered clear up to the early 1840s, when it began to suffer from inter-company competition and the indiscriminate trapping that had greatly reduced the beaver populations. Finally the industry received its death blow—delivered by a whim of style: The beaver hat was replaced in popularity by the silk hat!

During those years in which the fur trade had flourished, it was responsible for removing much of the unknown from the mysterious West, opening the way for the subsequent wave of westward expansion. It has given us tales of fascinating exploits and unique people who lived in ways that are still almost incomprehensible to us. And it has given us many of the geographic names in use today.

Jackson Hole was one of the places which received its name in this era, after several years of being merely "the Snake country." David E. Jackson was a trapper and partner in a fur company, with Jedediah Smith and William Sublette. It is thought that Sublette was the one who, in 1829, named the place "Jackson's Hole" and named its largest lake "Jackson's Lake." The lake had already been variously known as "Lake Biddle," "Lake Riddle," "Lewis Lake," and "Teton Lake," but the new name stuck—for both it and the valley. (The possessive endings have since been dropped.)

THE QUIET YEARS

After the extensive trapping activities ceased, little of consequence occured in the Teton country for nearly half a century. A few die-hard trappers sometimes waded the icy waters to set traps and retrieve beavers, but their catches were small and their value even smaller.

A few abortive attempts at mining were made. There is gold in Jackson Hole. It has been seen as a faint sheen on gravel beds beside the river. But it is "flour" gold, so fine it actually floats on water, and

Pronghorns (frequently called antelope), like humans, are the only species in their family. Both male and female pronghorns have real horns that are not shed each year, as are the antlers of deer and elk.

There is gold in Jackson Hole. It has been seen as a faint sheen on gravel beds beside the river. But it is "flour" gold, so fine it actually floats on water.

FRANK J. CAMENZIND

there is no economical way to collect it. But that didn't keep people from trying. And it encouraged them to search upriver for the source, the "mother lode." But each of the mining and prospecting ventures ended in failure.

Exploring parties sometimes passed through or around the Tetons. A member of one of these parties, Ferdinand Vandiveer Hayden, later led the official explorations of the Yellowstone country. Two other early explorers, Stevenson and Langford, later claimed the first ascent of the Grand Teton in 1872.

Meanwhile, the area was considered successively as part of the Oregon, Washington, Idaho, and Wyoming territories, but it had no residents to care one way or the other. The Sheepeaters certainly didn't. They still spent their summers at the campsite on Jackson Lake and would continue to do so until 1872, when they would accept the invi-

tation of their Shoshone kinsmen to join them on the Wind River Reservation—and their ancient culture would come to an end. The elk, too, still made their traditional, semiannual migrations through the valley. And the Teton Range continued to tower over the Snake River in the ancient quiet that also was soon to end.

Even the settlement of Jackson Hole was slow and peaceful. There was no boom to bring an instant influx of people, so expansion was gradual, one house at a time. John Holland, the first homesteader, arrived in 1884. The first post office was established in 1892, the first school in 1903, and the first newspaper in 1909. For a while the region was included in Uinta County of the Wyoming Territory; then for several years it was part of Lincoln County. It was not until 1921 that Teton County was established, with Jackson as the county seat, and then it was by special action of the Wyoming legislature because the new area did not meet either of the two requirements to become a county. It did not have a population of 3,000 or more, and it did not have a cumulative property value of $5 million or more.

Individual strife did sometimes occur in this isolated community. Idaho sheepmen were confronted and turned back at Teton Pass; two horse

ERWIN A. BAUER

Backpackers *on a mountain shoulder to the west of Phelps Lake scan the valley to the east. Grand Teton is truly a hiker's paradise!*

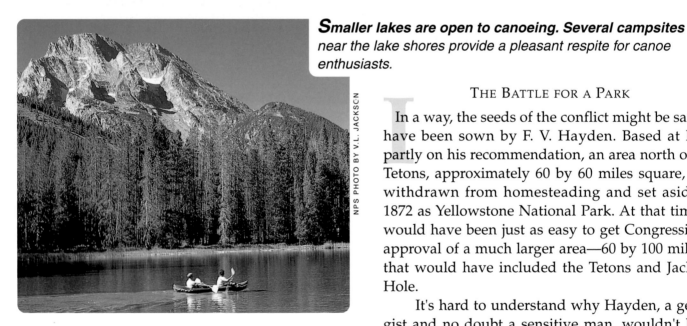

NPS PHOTO BY V.L. JACKSON

Smaller lakes are open to canoeing. Several campsites *near the lake shores provide a pleasant respite for canoe enthusiasts.*

thieves were shot; a miner killed his three partners; an Indian who was in custody as a poacher was killed during an attempted escape. So, all in all, Jackson can boast of a colorful past in the western tradition, including its fair share of bar brawls. But only one large-scale conflict took place here, and that one was political in nature. Its basis was the establishment and expansion of Grand Teton National Park.

THE BATTLE FOR A PARK

In a way, the seeds of the conflict might be said to have been sown by F. V. Hayden. Based at least partly on his recommendation, an area north of the Tetons, approximately 60 by 60 miles square, was withdrawn from homesteading and set aside in 1872 as Yellowstone National Park. At that time, it would have been just as easy to get Congressional approval of a much larger area—60 by 100 miles— that would have included the Tetons and Jackson Hole.

It's hard to understand why Hayden, a geologist and no doubt a sensitive man, wouldn't have wanted to incorporate the Teton Range in the new park. It wasn't because he was ignorant of its existence; he had seen the Tetons as a geologist with the Raynolds Expedition of 1860. Perhaps—and this may be hard for modern Americans to understand—interest was concentrated on Yellowstone only because of the oddity of its hydrothermal features, and since the Tetons had no such phenomena the area's importance was not recognized and it was passed over in the decisions to make neighboring Yellowstone a national park. Or perhaps the type of people who lived in the area—mountain men and western explorers—had seen and struggled across so many mountains that to them the

A trumpeter swan family glides sedately by.

The great horned owl guards his prey, a ruffed grouse.

The male sage grouse assumes a courtship pose.

An agile river otter seeks out fish in the Snake River.

Teton Range was just another barrier. But whatever the reason, the opportunity to set aside this magnificent scenic area as a national park was missed, and the stage was set for years of political squabbling.

Later Congressional attempts to enlarge Yellowstone toward the south failed, but efforts to establish a Yellowstone Timber Reserve in 1891 did succeed; this reserve subsequently became Teton National Forest, and when part of it was designated Grand Teton National Park in 1929, there was little local opposition. It didn't particularly matter

to the citizens of western Wyoming what the federal government called the various parts of its vast holdings there. Besides, the original park consisted only of the rugged mountains themselves and the lakes (except Jackson Lake)—all land that was no good for grazing and not very good, either, for hunting or timbering.

But those who had been campaigning for a national park felt that the one carved out of Forest Service land was only half a park. They felt it needed not only the dramatic Teton Range but also an unspoiled area from which to view it, a require-

ED COOPER

The Chapel of the Transfiguration was built in 1925 near Menor's Ferry, which was then the center of activity in central Jackson Hole. Regular Sunday services are held in the chapel in the summer, and has been a silent witness to many weddings over the past fifty years. Back in the 1890s, getting across Snake River was not always easy. Bill Menor built a ferry in 1892, which he operated until 1927 when a bridge was built.

ment that called for the acquisition of considerable acreage on the floor of Jackson Hole. And that prospect caused much apprehension and opposition from the local citizens and the people of Wyoming.

Some of the objections were purely economic, but most were based on the distrust that Westerners traditionally held for the federal government, based on the feeling that it catered to the concentration of people and money in the populous, industrial East. A significant number of Jackson Hole ranchers and other citizens, however, favored the expansion of Grand Teton National Park as offering the best hope for the economic and cultural future of their community.

As a result of the strong feelings and personalities involved, the struggle for park expansion was long and the issues complex. It was a period characterized by political manipulation, charges and counter-charges, insults and innuendo. But two men, Horace Albright and John D. Rockefeller, Jr., emerged from that conflict as having made lasting contributions to the national park concept.

Albright, in 1916 serving as assistant director of the newly created National Park Service, recognized the Teton potential and began to work for its preservation. His efforts continued for 34 years, including 10 years as superintendent of Yellowstone National Park and a term as director of the National Park Service. In 1926, Albright, as superintendent, was host to Mr. Rockefeller for his 12-day visit to Yellowstone. Albright conducted his

wealthy guest throughout the park and on south into Jackson Hole, and he infected Rockefeller with his own enthusiasm for a Teton park.

The next year Rockefeller turned this enthusiasm to action, by incorporating the Snake River Land Company for the purpose of buying private land to then be donated to the nation and made a part of Grand Teton National Park. In order to avoid the increase in selling prices that the Rockefeller name would no doubt have engendered, he kept his connection with the company secret. But this seemingly sensible business precaution backfired. When the ownership and purpose of the company finally became publicly known in 1930, it seemed to be proof of what Westerners had "known" all along   the federal government and eastern capital were guilty of connivance and collusion. A wave of protest swept the West, preventing for several years the acceptance of the generous Rockefeller gift and the enlargement of the park.

Another wave of protest followed in 1943, a result of the little understood statutory difference between a national park and a national monument. A park must be established by Congressional action, but a monument may be created by presidential proclamation. President Roosevelt signed such a proclamation in that year, creating Jackson Hole National Monument from various acreages of Forest Service land (including many acres of lake surface) and withdrawn public land. The Rockefeller gift of 32,170 acres was accepted as an addition to the monument in 1949.

That act was vigorously fought by Wyoming, in concert with most of the western states, traditionally at odds with Washington over land matters. But gradually, over the next seven years, opposition to the monument subsided, and in 1950 compromise solutions were reached; Congress disestablished Jackson Hole National Monument and incorporated its land into Grand Teton National Park. The "tyranny of the majority" had prevailed.

This happy cutthroat will live to see another day due to a fisherman's catch and release sporting adventure. The thrill is in the catch!

ERWIN & PEGGY BAUER

Fishing is an all season sport at Grand Teton. Winter can provide it all—cross-country skiing; being away from the crowds, undisturbed fishing. A beautiful vacation!

And, as it has so many times throughout the history of the United States, the majority opinion has proved sound. Jackson Hole is high and its climate is harsh, with a short growing season. Much of its soil is unsuited to either farming or ranching operations. Its beaver is a limited resource, and its minerals are not profitable to work. In fact, Jackson Hole has only two marketable products—incomparable scenery and a superb climate for winter sports. The area has successfully made the transition from an agricultural economy to an economy based on two-season tourism. In 1921, the whole of Teton County was valued at less than $5 million. Today, almost any square mile of Jackson Hole would be assessed at many more times that figure.

The reason is people, tourists, and new residents, and their appreciation of the grandeur and beauty of the natural world, a world that is now securely protected and preserved for the for- seeable future--Grand Teton National Park.

SUGGESTED READING

GILMORE, JACKIE. *in pictures Grand Teton The Continuing Story* Las Vegas, Nevada: KC Publications, Inc., 1995.

SAYLOR, DAVID J. *Jackson Hole, Wyoming: In the Shadow of the Tetons.* Norman, Oklahoma: University of Oklahoma Press, 1977.

ERWIN & PEGGY BAUER

Beneath the gaze of Mount Moran a fisherman enjoys the solitude of a quiet section of the Snake River—a time to refresh the mind and body.

All About Grand Teton National Park

Grand Teton Natural History Association

Grand Teton Natural History Association (GTNHA), founded in 1937, provides an ever-expanding number of interpretive and educational publications to visitors of Grand Teton National Park. With increased visitation, requests for association funding to augment federal budgets also increase. Profits from bookstores provide funding to Grand Teton National Park for renovation of visitor centers; printing expenses for the park newspaper, the *"Teewinot,"* and thousands of free maps and informational leaflets; exhibits in visitor centers and on trails; supplies for campfire programs; stipends for ranger-naturalist internships; and varied research projects.

COYOTE
ERWIN A. BAUER

GRAND TETON *Young Naturalist*

A Young Naturalist is a special and important individual. Young Naturalists learn the importance of taking care and protecting all of the animals, plant life, rocks and mountains. Young Naturalists watch moose, birds and other wildlife and look for animal tracks. They pick up litter and put it in the garbage can. Young Naturalists never feed wild animals in a national park. Young Naturalists know that national parks are special places that need to be protected, so that they will be just as special in the future.

To become a Young Naturalist is quite simple, all you have to do is read *The Grand Adventure Newspaper*, complete the fun and exciting activities and then bring your completed newspaper with a $1.00 donation to the Colter Bay, Moose or Jenny Lake Visitor Center. A ranger will ask you to take the Young Naturalist's pledge and award you a Young Naturalist patch.   Wear it with pride!

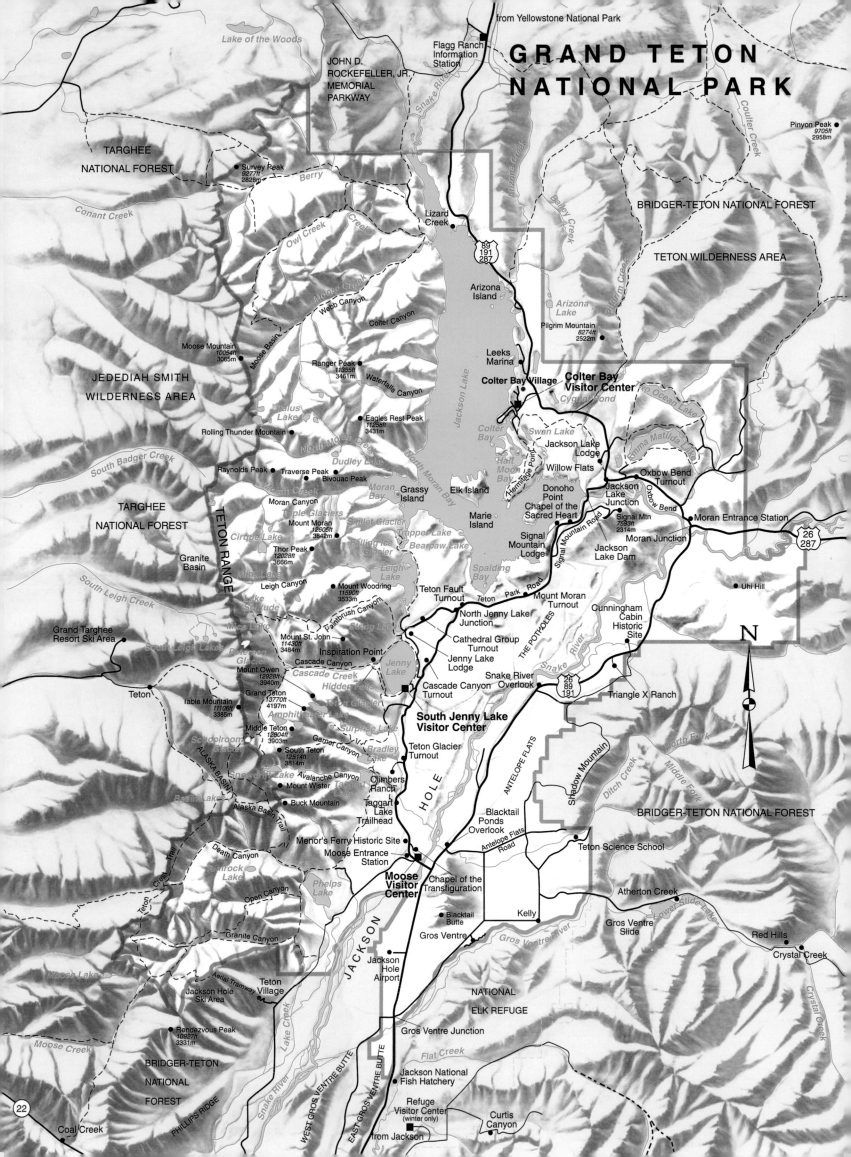

GRAND TETON NATIONAL PARK

from Yellowstone National Park

Flagg Ranch Information Station

JOHN D. ROCKEFELLER, JR. MEMORIAL PARKWAY

Lake of the Woods

TARGHEE NATIONAL FOREST

Survey Peak
9277ft
2828m

Berry Creek

Owl Creek

Conant Creek

Lizard Creek

Snake River

Arizona Creek

Bailey Creek

Pinyon Peak
9705ft
2958m

Coulter Creek

BRIDGER-TETON NATIONAL FOREST

TETON WILDERNESS AREA

Pilgrim Creek

89 191 287

Arizona Island

Arizona Lake

Webb Canyon

Moose Creek

Colter Canyon

Pilgrim Mountain
8274ft
2522m

JEDEDIAH SMITH WILDERNESS AREA

Moose Mountain
10054ft
3065m

Moose Basin

Ranger Peak
11355ft
3461m

Waterfalls Canyon

Leeks Marina

Colter Bay Village

Colter Bay Visitor Center

Cygnet Pond

Two Ocean Lake

Eagles Rest Peak
11258ft
3431m

Jackson Lake

Colter Bay

Swan Lake

Jackson Lake Lodge

Emma Matilda Lake

Rolling Thunder Mountain

Talus Lake

North Moran Canyon

Willow Flats

Oxbow Bend Turnout

Dudley Lake

Half Moon Bay

Hermitage Point

Jackson Lake Junction

Raynolds Peak

Traverse Peak

Bivouac Peak

Moran Bay

Grassy Island

Elk Island

Donoho Point

Chapel of the Sacred Heart

Oxbow Bend

Moran Entrance Station

TARGHEE NATIONAL FOREST

South Badger Creek

Moran Canyon

Triple Glaciers

Mount Moran
12605ft
3842m

Skillet Glacier

Trapper Lake

Marie Island

Signal Mtn
7593ft
2314m

Moran Junction

26 287

Granite Basin

Cirque Lake

Thor Peak
12028ft
3666m

Falling Ice Glacier

Bearpaw Lake

Spalding Bay

Signal Mountain Lodge

Jackson Lake Dam

Uhi Hill

TETON RANGE

Mink Lake

Leigh Canyon

Leigh Lake

Mount Woodring
11590ft
3533m

Teton Fault Turnout

Teton Park Road

Mount Moran Turnout

Signal Mountain Road

Cunningham Cabin Historic Site

South Leigh Creek

Lake Solitude

Mica Lake

Mount St. John
11430ft
3484m

Paintbrush Canyon

String Lake

North Jenny Lake Junction

Cathedral Group Turnout

THE POTHOLES

Snake River

Grand Targhee Resort Ski Area

South Leigh Lakes

Petersen Glacier

Inspiration Point

Cascade Canyon

Cascade Creek

Hidden Falls

Jenny Lake

Jenny Lake Lodge

Cascade Canyon Turnout

Snake River Overlook

26 89 191

Teton

Mount Owen
12928ft
3940m

Table Mountain
11106ft
3385m

Grand Teton
13770ft
4197m

Teton Glacier

South Jenny Lake Visitor Center

Triangle X Ranch

Amphitheater Lake

Middle Teton
12804ft
3903m

Surprise Lake

Bradley Lake

Teton Glacier Turnout

Garnet Canyon

ALASKA BASIN

Schoolroom Glacier

South Teton
12514ft
3814m

Snowdrift Lake

Avalanche Canyon

Mount Wister

Climbers Ranch

HOLE

ANTELOPE FLATS

Shadow Mountain

Ditch Creek

North Fork

BRIDGER-TETON NATIONAL FOREST

Basin Lake

Buck Mountain

Alaska Basin Trail

Taggart Lake

Taggart Lake Trailhead

Blacktail Ponds Overlook

Middle Fork

Death Canyon

Menor's Ferry Historic Site

Moose Entrance Station

Antelope Flats Road

Teton Science School

Lower Slide Lake

Shrock Lake

Teton Crest Trail

Moose Visitor Center

Chapel of the Transfiguration

Atherton Creek

Phelps Lake

Blacktail Butte

Kelly

Gros Ventre Slide

Open Canyon

Gros Ventre

Red Hills

JACKSON

Granite Canyon

Gros Ventre River

Crystal Creek

Lake Creek

Jackson Hole Airport

Aerial Tramway Road

Teton Village

NATIONAL

Rendezvous Peak
10927ft
3331m

Jackson Hole Ski Area

ELK REFUGE

Moose Lake

Moose Creek

BRIDGER-TETON NATIONAL FOREST

PHILLIPS RIDGE

WEST GROS VENTRE BUTTE

EAST GROS VENTRE BUTTE

Gros Ventre Junction

Flat Creek

Jackson National Fish Hatchery

Refuge Visitor Center (winter only)

Curtis Canyon

Coal Creek

from Jackson

N

A Look to the Future

A park is for people! The whole park idea was conceived because it was needed by our society, and it must be maintained in a condition as natural as possible in order to serve that need. Grand Teton—and all our National Parks must continue to reduce the impact of visitors, upon the area and upon each other.

To do so, we need innovative ideas and practices that will allow for increased use of the park without lessening the quality of the Teton experience.

We understand better now that our national parks are not simply for recreation. They are also for restoration—body, mind and spirit. We are learning a new attitude—an attitude that will allow us to stand before the spires of the Cathedral Group with the same courtesy and respect that we have learned to display in other, man-made cathedrals.

Our grandchildren will share these natural marvels with millions of people. If they should leave Grand Teton National Park feeling as inspired and rewarded as we have then we have succeeded as keepers of a monumental and a precious trust.

JOHN P. GEORGE

Cloaked in fall color the Teton peak stands with a majesty fitting to be called Grand.

KC Publications has been the leading publisher of colorful, interpretive books about National Park areas, public lands, Indian lands, and related subjects for over 40 years. We have 6 active series—over 135 titles—with Translation Packages in up to 8 languages for over half the areas we cover. Write, call, or visit our web site for our full-color catalog.

Our series are:

The Story Behind the Scenery® – Compelling stories of over 65 National Park areas and similar Public Land areas. Some with Translation Packages.

*in pictures... **The Continuing Story**®* – A companion, pictorially oriented, series on America's National Parks. All titles have Translation Packages.

For Young Adventurers™ – Dedicated to young seekers and keepers of all things wild and sacred. Explore America's Heritage from A to Z.

Voyage of Discovery® – Exploration of the expansion of the western United States.

Indian Culture and the Southwest – All about Native Americans, past and present.

Calendars – For National Parks in dramatic full color, and a companion Color Your Own series, with crayons.

To receive our full-color catalog featuring over 135 titles—Books, Calendars, Screen Scenes, Videos, Audio Tapes, and other related specialty products:

Call (800-626-9673), fax (702-433-3420), write to the address below, Or visit our web site at www.kcpublications.com

Published by KC Publications, 3245 E. Patrick Ln., Suite A, Las Vegas, NV 89120.

Inside back cover: The Snake River and its banks are a separate ecosystem that includes a complex variety of life. Photo by Ed Cooper

Back cover: Snowy Teton Spires. Photo by John P. George

Created, Designed, and Published in the U.S.A.
Printed by Tien Wah Press (Pte.) Ltd, Singapore
Pre-Press by United Graphic Pte. Ltd